Original title:
Verses in Architecture

Copyright © 2024 Creative Arts Management OÜ
All rights reserved.

Author: Tim Wood
ISBN HARDBACK: 978-9916-88-076-0
ISBN PAPERBACK: 978-9916-88-077-7

Harmony in Hard Lines

In shadows deep, where whispers blend,
A melody begins to mend.
With every note, the heart takes flight,
A symphony born from darkest night.

Amidst the storms, we find our peace,
As chaos swirls, our doubts release.
The earth may tremble, the skies may roar,
Yet love remains, forever more.

Threads of silver in tangled threads,
We weave our dreams, where hope now spreads.
In every challenge, a lesson lies,
For from the cracks, new beauty rises.

So let the hard lines draw their course,
For in each struggle, we find our force.
With hands united, we stand tall,
In harmony's embrace, we shall not fall.

The Solidity of Serenity

In quiet corners, shadows play,
The sun dips low, embracing day.
Whispers float through the gentle breeze,
Finding peace in rustling leaves.

Stillness wraps the world in grace,
Each moment here, a sacred space.
The heartbeat slows, the mind unwinds,
In solitude, true calm one finds.

Soft echoes of the evening's glow,
The stars above begin to show.
Threads of silence weave the night,
In this embrace, all feels right.

The Call of the Cornice

Above the streets, where dreams ignite,
A cornice crowns the building's height.
It whispers tales of times gone by,
Of love and laughter, a gentle sigh.

A lifeline to the past it shows,
In shadows cast where history flows.
Each curve and edge, a story told,
In every crevice, treasures hold.

The city breathes beneath the stars,
Its pulse reflected in the scars.
The call of cornice, bold and grand,
Awakens spirits in this land.

Whispering Walls

In ancient halls where secrets sleep,
The walls hold promises we keep.
Soft murmurs blend with time's own thread,
Tales of hearts that once were wed.

Each brick a witness, proud and true,
To laughter shared and shadows grew.
Whispering echoes, soft and low,
Remind us of all we used to know.

Through cracks and crevices they sigh,
Stories of love that cannot die.
The walls embrace, they listen well,
Guardians of the tales they tell.

Tenderness in Texture

The fabric soft against the skin,
A gentle touch, where dreams begin.
Threads intertwine, a dance so sweet,
In every fiber, warmth we meet.

Silken whispers, a lover's caress,
Textures play, feelings express.
In woven moments, hearts take flight,
Bathed in the glow of soft twilight.

Linen hugs in the morning light,
Bringing joy, chasing the night.
Tenderness wrapped in every seam,
Life, a beautiful woven dream.

Spheres of Serenity

In gentle ripples, calm unfolds,
A tranquil space where stillness holds.
Beneath the sky, where dreams arise,
The heart finds peace, the spirit flies.

Whispers of nature softly weave,
A tapestry that helps us believe.
In every breath, a moment sweet,
In every heart, where rhythms meet.

The light that dances on the lake,
Reflects the joy that we all make.
In silence deep, our thoughts take flight,
In Spheres of Serenity, pure delight.

Together here, we find our grace,
In quietude, we find our place.
Wrapped in warmth, we feel the love,
As gentle winds kiss skies above.

An Ode to Openings

With every dawn, a fresh start blooms,
Bright horizons chase away the glooms.
Each new path beckons, calls to be,
An adventure waits; new sights to see.

Doors creak open, revealing light,
A world of wonder, vibrant and bright.
The heart leaps forth, unbound, alive,
In An Ode to Openings, we thrive.

Choices laid like petals unfurl,
Inviting hope to dance and twirl.
In brave pursuit, our dreams ignite,
In every moment, the future's bright.

So here we stand, at the divide,
Embracing change with arms open wide.
Each step we take, a promise made,
In the realm of beginnings, unafraid.

The Lyrical Layout

On paper white, the words do dance,
In rhythmic flow, they weave romance.
A canvas blank now comes alive,
With strokes of ink, ideas thrive.

Here sonnets rise and stories spin,
Within these lines, the magic begins.
Each phrase, a note in harmony,
In The Lyrical Layout, we are free.

Verses sing and stanzas play,
Each syllable crafted in a careful way.
Emotions wrapped in lines so tight,
A symphony of thoughts takes flight.

Join in the joy of crafted verse,
In every poem, the universe.
The beauty blooms where hearts engage,
In the lyrical embrace of the page.

Chambers of Contemplation

In quiet rooms where shadows play,
Thoughts drift softly, night and day.
Reflections whisper on the wall,
In Chambers of Contemplation, we stall.

Time pauses here, a gentle breath,
In stillness, we confront our depth.
With every sigh, we search for truth,
Recalling dreams from our youth.

The mind unwinds, a tapestry,
Of lessons learned and memories free.
Each corner holds a secret bare,
In this embrace, we lay ourselves bare.

In solitude, we find the light,
With open hearts, we take our flight.
So linger long, let silence reign,
In these chambers, peace remains.

The Silence of Spaces

In corners where no words remain,
The stillness breathes a soft refrain.
Empty echoes linger near,
Where time forgets and shadows cheer.

Beneath the weight of unseen air,
A quiet hum, a whispered prayer.
Walls hold secrets, deep and wide,
In silence, all its dreams abide.

The light that dares to filter through,
Dances gently, touching hue.
In this void, a heart does soar,
Finding peace in nevermore.

Echoes of Stone

A rugged path, old stones align,
Hushed whispers from the bramble vine.
In ancient halls where shadows creep,
The stories of the past still seep.

Each step upon this weathered ground,
A tale of loss, a mournful sound.
The echoes carry, soft yet bold,
Of battles fought and legends told.

In twilight's glow, the silence fades,
While memories dance in dusty glades.
The stone holds all, in quiet grace,
A tapestry of time and space.

Shadows on the Facade

Against the wall, dark forms take flight,
In fleeting glimpses of day and night.
Layers of dusk and dawning light,
A canvas painted in hushed fright.

Each silhouette tells tales untold,
Of dreams once bright and hearts grown cold.
The facade stands in quiet strife,
A witness to the dance of life.

As twilight drapes its velvet cloak,
A silence wraps, the shadows smoke.
Within the folds, the whispers play,
Tangled stories fade away.

Whispers within the Walls

Between each brick, a voice resides,
With every crack, a secret hides.
The whispers linger, soft and low,
Tracing stories of long ago.

In hushed tones, the past unfolds,
As time erodes both young and old.
Within the beams, the frail threads weave,
A tapestry, hearts won't leave.

Footsteps echo in the night,
As shadows dance in muted light.
In this embrace, I find my place,
Where whispers of the walls interlace.

Rhapsody in Brick

In the heart of the city, bricks align,
Stories whispered in each defined line,
Colors blend in a beautiful mess,
Echoes of laughter, time's soft caress.

Beneath the gray skies, hope still glows,
Mossy crevices where nature grows,
Each brick a memory, strong and bold,
Tales of the past in their silence told.

Windows frame dreams of lives long gone,
Casting shadows as daylight dawns,
In the creak of the door, you may find,
The rhapsody echoing within the mind.

Arches of Memory

Beneath the arches, time stands still,
Whispers of yesteryears, soft and shrill,
Each curve a journey, a story unfurled,
Binding the past to the present world.

Sunlight dances through towering heights,
Casting spells of golden delights,
Moments captured in silence and stone,
Where the echoes of laughter are never alone.

Worn footsteps tell of love and loss,
Sacred paths weaved across the gloss,
In the shadows, memories blend,
An archway's embrace, where journeys end.

The Poetry of Horizon Lines

Where earth meets sky, dreams take flight,
Colors collide in fading light,
Horizons stretch, a canvas vast,
Whispers of futures, echoes of past.

Every sunrise, a poem anew,
Painting the world in luminous hue,
Waves of the ocean rise and dive,
In the hush of twilight, we come alive.

Beneath the stars, our hopes ignite,
In the darkness, we find our light,
Across the horizon, boundless space,
The poetry of life in each embrace.

Walls That Speak

Walls adorned with stories untold,
Each crack and crevice, a glimpse of gold,
Paintings of laughter, tears, and strife,
In their silence, they echo life.

Hands that have touched, left their mark,
Layers of paint, a journey's spark,
Every hue a whisper, every shade a song,
In the heart of the city, where we all belong.

From the rooftops to the ground, they stand,
Guardians of dreams, both quiet and grand,
Listening closely, secrets they keep,
In the stillness of night, the walls still speak.

Geometry of Emotion

In angles sharp, our feelings meet,
Measured lines beneath our feet.
A constellation of desires,
Drawing paths where love inspires.

Circles spin in silent grace,
Tracing curves of time and space.
In every shape, a story told,
Of friendships bright and hearts of gold.

Triangles hold the weight of pain,
Where two sides work to break the chain.
A balance sought in every form,
Through juxtaposed hearts we transform.

The Heartbeat of Design

With every sketch, a pulse begins,
In lines where passion finds its wins.
Colors dance to a silent beat,
Crafting beauty, raw and sweet.

Templates laid and dreams defined,
In symmetry, our souls entwined.
Textures speak in whispers low,
As each design begins to glow.

From chaos springs the ordered thought,
In every project, battles fought.
The heartbeat echoes through each space,
Creating harmony, leaving trace.

Echo Chamber of Existence

In mirrored walls, a voice is found,
Reflections stretch, a world around.
Whispers bounce within our minds,
In every echo, truth unwinds.

Thoughts collide in endless flight,
In chambers dark, there's only light.
Consciousness, a spiraled dance,
Echoing chance in a fleeting glance.

Time reverberates, lives entwine,
In cycles, fate and design.
To exist is to resonate,
In echoes shared, we motivate.

Blueprints of the Mind

In sketches vague, ideas bloom,
Blueprints drawn in faded room.
Imagination paves the way,
For dreams to build their bold display.

Foundations laid in thoughts we share,
Constructing hopes with utmost care.
In every plan, our vision grows,
As seeds of passion intertwine, expose.

Walls of doubt may rise and fail,
Yet we persist, our dreams unveil.
With every stroke, we design life,
In blueprints drawn, we conquer strife.

Shadows on the Facade

In twilight's grasp, the shadows creep,
Soft whispers roam where silence sleeps.
Shapes dance along the crumbling wall,
Secrets linger, only dusk can call.

Figures merge in the fading light,
Echoes of past in the heart of night.
Windows blink with a knowing tease,
Breath of the lost in the evening breeze.

A game of forms on the surface played,
Fleeting glimpses of joy and shade.
Faces hidden, stories untold,
In shadows deep, the truth unfolds.

The Language of Light and Space

In every beam that gently breaks,
A silent song the cosmos makes.
Stars twinkle in a vast ballet,
Guiding lost dreams along their way.

A shimmer here, a glow up high,
Painting hope across the sky.
Light whispers soft in colors bright,
Translating the depths of dark to light.

Across the expanse, the universe speaks,
In cosmic rhythms, the spirit seeks.
Each ray a message, each shadow a story,
In the dance of realms, we find our glory.

Foundations of Thought

Deep in the mind, ideas take form,
Waves of insight in chaos swarm.
Thoughts erupt like a summer's storm,
Building bridges where notions can warm.

Words like bricks, they stack and rise,
Crafting castles, reaching the skies.
Each notion stands on another's ground,
In the silence, their truth is found.

Yet shadows linger, doubts interlace,
In the labyrinth, we wander, we chase.
Foundations shake, but persist we must,
In thoughts we nurture, in dreams we trust.

Windows to the Soul

Glimmers of truth in soft gazes lie,
A clarity deep, where secrets fry.
Each glance a chapter, a hidden scroll,
Reflecting the depths, the windows to the soul.

Mirrored emotions, in silence abide,
A dance in the light where feelings hide.
Eyes weave tales of joy and of woe,
Through these portals, our spirits flow.

Navigating love, with each tender look,
Scripted in stars, in the pages of a book.
Within every gaze, a universe stirs,
Boundless and bright, in all that occurs.

Canvassed Corners

In corners where shadows play,
A whisper of colors sway.
Brushstrokes dance, vivid and bright,
Fleeting moments, a pure delight.

Each canvas tells a hidden tale,
With swirls and strokes that unveil.
Framed within a wooden crest,
Art speaks softly, never rests.

Textures mingle, smooth and rough,
Every detail, layered stuff.
In the silence, visions bloom,
Filling hearts, dispelling gloom.

From corner to corner, we explore,
Endless wonders we adore.
A journey through hues and lines,
In canvassed corners, beauty shines.

The Art of Ascent

Step by step, we rise anew,
Chasing dreams in skies so blue.
With each heartbeat, hopes ignite,
The summit calls, a tempting sight.

We climb the paths of jagged stone,
In courage, we are not alone.
The wind whispers secrets bold,
Of those who dared and stories told.

Hands reach out to grasp the air,
As hearts embrace the thrill of dare.
With every breath, we feel alive,
In the art of ascent, we thrive.

When we crest that final peak,
The world below becomes less bleak.
Beyond the clouds, in endless space,
The journey ends, a warm embrace.

Journey Through Geometry

Shapes align in perfect harmony,
Drawing paths, a sweet symphony.
Circles spin and triangles soar,
In this realm, we seek for more.

Angles sharp, like thoughts in flight,
Crafting dreams both day and night.
Lines converge, a dance so bold,
Telling stories yet untold.

With every vertex, we explore,
The essence of what lies in store.
Through dimensions vast and wide,
In geometry, we take our stride.

Patterns weave a tapestry bright,
Guiding us towards the light.
Every shape, a tale to spin,
In this journey, we begin.

Landscapes of Light

Golden rays touch the rolling hills,
Painting the sky with tranquil thrills.
Sunset whispers, colors blend,
In landscapes of light, we transcend.

Morning breaks with silken hues,
Waking dreams in vibrant views.
Each moment captured, a fleeting sight,
In nature's grasp, pure delight.

Clouds embrace the sun's warm glow,
Casting shadows where rivers flow.
Reflections dance on waters bright,
Creating landscapes bathed in light.

As nightfall drapes its velvet cloak,
Stars arise and softly poke.
In every glimmer, dreams take flight,
Eternal tales in landscapes of light.

Emotions Encased

In a jar, a tear, a smile,
Captured moments, held awhile.
Whispers of joy, shadows of pain,
Each drop a story, a heart's refrain.

Laughter echoes in the night air,
Hopeful dreams tossed everywhere.
Fleeting glances, memories fade,
In the silence, love is made.

Bottled sunlight, shades of blue,
The weight of hearts, so strong, so true.
Fragile vessels holding our fears,
Emotions encased through all the years.

Syllables in Skylines

Silhouettes graze the twilight,
Words dance in the dimming light.
Verses rise like towers tall,
Beneath the stars, we hear their call.

Each consonant a brick laid strong,
Vowels echo in the throng.
Stanzas flow like rivers wide,
Painting cities, turning tide.

Sketching dreams upon the breeze,
Lines entwining through the trees.
Syllables soar, horizons chase,
In every curve, we find a place.

The Poetry of Places

Concrete jungles whisper low,
Every street tells tales we know.
Sidewalks speak of hurried feet,
Every pause, a heartbeat sweet.

Mountains echo ancient lore,
Valleys sigh with memories stored.
Rivers hum a constant tune,
Underneath the silver moon.

Sunsets drape the world in gold,
Winds weave stories yet untold.
In every corner, life does bloom,
The poetry of places—an endless room.

Windows to Wonder

Framed by glass, a view so clear,
Each scene alive, inviting near.
Children play beneath the sun,
Life unfolds, a web begun.

Raindrops race on panes so bright,
Mirroring dreams in shades of light.
Seasons change, the frame remains,
Offering glimpses, joy, and pains.

Through these windows, worlds collide,
A canvas where our hearts confide.
In every glance, a chance to see,
The wonder of what's yet to be.

Landmarks of Legacy

In the shadow of great stones,
History whispers low,
Tales of those who walked,
Paths of courage, we follow.

Each monument, a beacon,
Standing proud through the years,
Marking time's relentless march,
Witness to hopes and fears.

Roots entwined with the soil,
Legends carved in the air,
Reminders of where we've come,
Stories shared, laid bare.

Legacies etched in silence,
Foundations of dreams unfold,
A tapestry of the past,
In every heart, we hold.

The Aesthetic Alchemy

Brush strokes blend in harmony,
Colors dance on the canvas,
Visions glow with energy,
Capturing fleeting moments.

Shapes entwined, an artisan's grip,
Crafting dreams in shades so bright,
Light and shadow in a trip,
Turning darkness into light.

Each piece tells a story,
Merging passion with design,
In the realm of imagination,
Boundless and divine.

Sculpted dreams take their form,
In silence, they express,
An alchemical rebirth,
In beauty, we find rest.

Strokes of Straight Lines

Edges sharp and angles clear,
Precision in every move,
Designs that captivate the eye,
Geometry in a groove.

Lines that lead the heart and mind,
Structure sings in each form,
A balance of beauty defined,
In every curve, a norm.

Architects of space and light,
Spaces breathe with intention,
Foundations built, touching sky,
A vision, our invention.

In the order, chaos finds,
The art of simple grace,
Strokes of straight lines whisper truth,
In this crafted space.

The Dance of Design

Shapes entwined in gentle flow,
Movement brings the still to life,
Threads of creativity sewn,
In the rhythm of the strife.

Patterns swirl like a soft breeze,
Unraveling stories unfold,
Every twist and turn at ease,
In shadows, secrets told.

The canvas breathes with each sway,
A harmony of form and space,
Each creation finds its way,
In this timeless embrace.

Design, a dance of light and thought,
Where dreams and visions twine,
A celebration, gently sought,
In every line, we shine.

Porches to the Past

Old swings creak with time,
Whispers of laughter remain,
Photos fade like the sun,
Memories dance through the rain.

Wooden steps worn and gray,
Each knot tells a tale,
Breezes carry our sighs,
In silence, they prevail.

Garden blooms often sigh,
Colors blend with the dusk,
Echoes of lives gone by,
Each shadow holds its husk.

Sunset drapes the porch light,
As twilight starts to play,
We sit with ghosts tonight,
In their company, we stay.

Elegies of Elevation

Clouds cradle the peaks high,
Mountains wear a crown of white,
Breezes sing to the sky,
Whispers born of purest light.

Valleys dip in shadowed grace,
Echoes linger in the air,
Footsteps lead to space,
Where souls breathe without a care.

Summits reach for the stars,
Memories linger like dew,
In this world full of scars,
The heart always finds its view.

Each ascent holds a promise,
In the stillness, we find,
Every struggle a chorus,
To the heights, we are blind.

The Rhythm of Rebar

Steel ribs weave through the sky,
Structures breathe in design,
Workers hum as they tie,
Strength forged in every line.

Cement flows like a dream,
Foundations deep and wide,
With each sturdy beam,
More than a home, a pride.

Life arises from blueprints,
Hopes held in every bolt,
Progress sings in its hints,
In this, we feel our jolt.

In the heart of the city,
Where shadows softly blend,
Steel and dreams in committee,
A rhythm that won't end.

Stairways to Soliloquy

Steps echo in the night,
Whispers of thoughts ascend,
Each rise brings new insight,
Dreams and fears softly blend.

Candles flicker in halls,
Light dances on each tread,
Voices of memory calls,
In the dark, stories spread.

Landing soft like a sigh,
Moments frozen in place,
In silence, we rely,
On shadows to embrace.

These stairways lead us home,
To corners of our mind,
In solitude, we roam,
Where true selves are defined.

Odyssey of the Overhang

Beneath the eaves, the shadows creep,
Whispers of tales, in silence deep.
Branches sway with secrets to share,
Nature's canvas, finely laid bare.

Winds weave through the aging wood,
Echoes of journeys, misunderstood.
Time stands still, the moments blend,
In the overhang, where stories mend.

Light breaks softly, casting gold,
Dreams unfold, both brave and bold.
Up above, the sky reveals,
A tapestry of fate that heals.

In this realm of hanging grace,
We find our fears, we find our place.
Thus we wander, together drawn,
Through the twilight, we greet the dawn.

Rhyme of the Roof

Upon the shingles, raindrops play,
A melody that drifts away.
Each note a part of the storm's embrace,
Whirling whispers in this sacred space.

Under the arches, dreams ignite,
Softly glowing in the night.
Crickets chirp a soothing tune,
Beneath the gaze of a watchful moon.

Every tile holds a memory dear,
Stories woven, year by year.
As seasons change and time will flow,
The rhyme of the roof begins to grow.

In silence waits the woven spell,
Where echoes of laughter often dwell.
Through every storm and gentle breeze,
The roof enchants, our hearts it frees.

Chronicles of Columns

Stand tall, the columns rise with pride,
Guardians of secrets they provide.
Marble whispers from ages past,
Holding stories that forever last.

In the stillness, the echoes speak,
Wisdom flows, yet time feels weak.
Each groove a chapter, worn and grand,
A testament of time's own hand.

Beneath their shade, we dream anew,
Linking the old with the bright and true.
As sunlight dances with shadow's grace,
We strive to find our rightful place.

A pillar stands for hope and doubt,
In every heart, a sacred shout.
Chronicles whispered by the stones,
In unity, we find our bones.

Sculpted Silence

In the stillness, a moment carved,
Where echoes of the past are starved.
Shapes emerge from fog and time,
Sculpted silence, a quiet rhyme.

The rock seems to breathe, to sigh,
As shadows dance and wander by.
With every curve, a tale unfolds,
Of aching dreams and visions bold.

In gentle hands, the beauty sways,
Chiseled whispers of bygone days.
Each silence sings a song profound,
In sculpted art, our souls are found.

So here we stand, in quiet awe,
Beneath the gaze of nature's law.
Sculpted silence, a sacred space,
Where time stands still and hearts embrace.

The Language of Lines

In whispers traced on paper's skin,
Words dance like shadows, soft and thin.
Each letter carved in silent grace,
A tapestry woven in time and space.

From curves that bend to angles sharp,
Every line a note, a silent harp.
Languages breach with strokes so light,
A symphony born of ink and flight.

Through scribbled dreams and fractured thought,
The beauty of lines cannot be caught.
They speak in hues of vivid hue,
In every twist, a story new.

So let us write, let fingers glide,
In the language of lines where hearts confide.
An endless journey, forever bright,
In every stroke, we ignite the light.

Pillars of Poetry

With every verse, a pillar stands,
Supporting dreams with gentle hands.
Crafted in moments, cherished and bold,
Stories of silence and secrets told.

Each stanza holds a tender weight,
Building bridges, connecting fate.
In rhythmic beats, stories unfold,
Words like stones in structures of gold.

The power of verse, a force unseen,
Shapes the world, serene yet keen.
With every quill, a fortress blooms,
Pillars of poetry conquer gloom.

In echoes of stanzas, we find our place,
Entwined in the beauty of shared space.
Together we rise, forever entwined,
As pillars of poetry, we redefine.

Symphonies in Steel

In the heart of the city, steel beams soar,
Creating a symphony, forevermore.
Each note a clang, a rhythm so true,
With echoes of labor, bright and new.

The whispers of workers, hands rough and worn,
Constructing dreams from dusk till dawn.
Melodies rise in the bustling street,
A chorus of hearts beneath their feet.

With every spark from the welder's flame,
The pulse of the city, a vibrant name.
Structures stand tall like notes in the sky,
Their beauty a song as time passes by.

In symphonies woven with threads of might,
The city resonates, pure delight.
A testament to strength and grace,
In symphonies of steel, we find our place.

Geometry of Grace

In angles acute, in circles spun,
The dance of lines has just begun.
Geometry whispers in curves divine,
A pattern of beauty that's purely mine.

Triangles rise, bold and bright,
Balanced in harmony, pure delight.
Each shape reveals a hidden truth,
In the heart's geometry, finds its youth.

With symmetry's charm and fractals' allure,
The geometry of grace feels so pure.
Canons of nature embrace the art,
Weaving connections that touch the heart.

In every corner, in every fold,
The world's geometry is a story told.
Embracing the shapes that life creates,
In the geometry of grace, love resonates.

A Palette of Perspectives

Colors blend in skies so bright,
Whispers shared in morning light.
Each hue tells a story true,
In the heart of me and you.

From crimson dawn to ocean's blue,
Every shade holds memories too.
Brush of life, both soft and bold,
A tapestry of dreams retold.

Through valleys low and mountains high,
We paint the world, both you and I.
In every glance, in every sigh,
A canvas where our thoughts will fly.

So let us blend with courage wide,
And in this art, let hope reside.
For in the palette we define,
The beauty of our hearts entwined.

Interludes of Infrastructure

Bridges arch in silent grace,
Connecting hearts, a warm embrace.
Steel and stone, the city's veins,
Whisper tales of hopes and pains.

Roads that stretch, ambitious and long,
Guide the journeys where we belong.
Minds entwine in the urban maze,
As life unfolds in bustling ways.

Pillars rise, a strong refrain,
Holding dreams while soft rains gain.
In every corner, shadows cast,
Chronicles of futures past.

So let us walk these paths we've paved,
In interludes, the dreams we've braved.
Infrastructure of a human heart,
Building bridges, playing our part.

Heartbeats in Hollow Spaces

Silent rooms where echoes dwell,
In whispered thoughts, we weave our spell.
Heartbeats soft in empty halls,
In solitude, the spirit calls.

Walls that hold both grief and joy,
Memories of each girl and boy.
In hollow spaces, stories breathe,
As time unravels, hearts believe.

Gentle sighs and fleeting dreams,
In vacant places, nothing seems.
Yet in the quiet, truths emerge,
With each heartbeat, life's old surge.

So let us fill these hollow shapes,
With laughter, love, and warm landscapes.
For even in the empty trace,
We find our solace, our embrace.

Timeless Towers

Towers rise against the sky,
Whispers echo, centuries fly.
Stone and glass in layered grace,
Marking time in every space.

History gleams in sunlit streaks,
In every brick, a secret speaks.
Guardians of dreams, they stand so tall,
Witness to the rise and fall.

In shadows long and futures cast,
Timeless towers hold fast.
With every sunset, they renew,
A legacy of what is true.

So let us stand and gaze with pride,
At those who dreamed and never hide.
For in their heights, we find the way,
To build our hope, to seize the day.

Stairways to Imagination

Steps that rise, painted bright,
Whispers of dreams in the night.
Each twist and turn unfolds a tale,
Where thoughts take flight, where hearts sail.

Shadows dance on the walls,
Creativity beckons and calls.
With every ascent, new worlds appear,
Stairways to vision, vivid and clear.

Moments captured in fleeting light,
As visions soar, take wondrous flight.
The echoes of laughter fill the air,
Imagination blooms, beyond compare.

A journey painted in hues of gold,
Stories waiting to be told.
On stairways built from dreams so grand,
We walk together, hand in hand.

The Rhythm of Roofs

Underneath the stars so bright,
Roofs hum softly in the night.
Each angle sways, an urban dance,
A symphony born from chance.

Tiles of terracotta and slate,
Whisper secrets of love and fate.
With each beat, a heart takes flight,
The rhythm flows, pure delight.

Gables rise in harmony,
A tune that echoes, wild and free.
Blending stories of all who dwell,
In this city, where dreams compel.

Patterns woven into the sky,
Inviting us to laugh and cry.
The rhythm pulses, strong and true,
In every roof, a world anew.

Metaphors in Mortar

Brick by brick, we build our dreams,
Metaphors woven in silent schemes.
The mortar binds with tales untold,
In every layer, courage bold.

Walls that whisper of love's embrace,
Hardships faced, yet we find grace.
Mortar mixed with blood and sweat,
A legacy we won't forget.

Stories etched in every crack,
Foundations strong, we won't look back.
This structure stands through storm and strife,
A tapestry of our shared life.

In every arch and every beam,
Flows the essence of a dream.
Metaphors rise, solid and true,
In mortar's grip, we find anew.

Canvases of the City

Streets painted in colors bold,
Stories of young and old are told.
Every corner, a brushstroke fine,
The city breathes, a work divine.

Graffiti dances on the walls,
Echoing life in vibrant calls.
Murals bright with tales of lore,
A canvas rich, forevermore.

Tall buildings stand like towering art,
Their silhouettes, a beating heart.
Windows glimmer like stars at night,
Reflecting dreams, pure delight.

In this gallery of brick and stone,
Creativity finds a home.
The city's pulse, a rhythmic show,
Canvases where imaginations grow.

Blueprinted Dreams

In quiet rooms where visions dwell,
Plans unfold like tales to tell.
Each stroke of pencil, seeds of light,
Hopes take flight in endless night.

Futures crafted, shapes align,
With every curve, a life divine.
Imagined worlds in whispers soar,
Foundations set, we dream of more.

Lines of purpose, drawn with care,
Life's designs float in the air.
From blueprints rise the paths we seek,
In dreams we find the words to speak.

With heart and hand, we sketch our fate,
Each dream a door we choose to create.
Through night's embrace, our spirits blend,
In blueprints, journeys never end.

Echoes of Design

In shadows cast by ancient stone,
Whispers of art remind us we're not alone.
Every curve, a story spun,
Echoes of design, in silence run.

Through halls where history resides,
Blueprints of dreams beneath the tides.
Sketches linger where light and dark meet,
Threads of thought, a rhythmic beat.

In the dance of form and space,
Echoes resonate, time's gentle embrace.
A world designed in muted hues,
Where heart and mind craft life's reviews.

From echoes past, we build anew,
In every line, a view so true.
In this canvas, our paths unwind,
With echoes of design, we're intertwined.

The Canvas of Concrete

Each slab a story, each wall a dream,
Within the city's ceaseless gleam.
Concrete whispers of hearts laid bare,
A canvas born from care and dare.

Brushstrokes bold in urban hues,
Pavements echo our silent views.
Structures rise to kiss the sky,
In this tableau, ambitions fly.

Textures tell of lives once led,
Foundations grounded, visions spread.
With every frame, we shape a tale,
The canvas of concrete will prevail.

As rain falls soft on asphalt streets,
The art of living pulses and beats.
In bricks and mortar, a life portrayed,
On this canvas, dreams are laid.

Arches of Time

Beneath the arches, shadows play,
Time's gentle hand leads us astray.
In every curve, a memory flows,
The past lives here, the present glows.

With each step, the echoes sing,
Of ages past and future's wing.
Guided by light, we walk the line,
In archways woven, our lives entwine.

Stories etched in stone and beam,
Time's embrace, a flowing stream.
Moments caught, like whispers shared,
In arches of time, we are bared.

Through bustling crowds, we find our way,
Bound by the past, come what may.
In these structures, we hold a rhyme,
Together we thrive, in arches of time.

Lullabies of the Landscape

Whispers of willows sway in the breeze,
Gentle sighs of hills in tranquil ease.
The river hums a soft, soothing song,
While stars twinkle, where night crowds belong.

Butterflies dance through fields of gold,
As sunlight unfolds secrets untold.
Meadows echo with laughter so bright,
Nature's embrace, a heart's pure delight.

Clouds wander lazily, painting the sky,
Dreams drift along, they quietly lie.
Shadows of trees stretch long on the ground,
In these sweet moments, peace can be found.

Glimmers of twilight begin to emerge,
A tapestry woven with nature's urge.
In lullabies sung by the land's gentle hand,
We find ourselves cradled, forever we stand.

Mosaics of Meaning

Fragments of thoughts like broken glass,
Reflecting stories of futures and past.
Each shard holds a piece of our shared truth,
In colors so vivid, igniting our youth.

Words swirl and coil, a dance of the mind,
Patterns emerge, both complex and kind.
In silence, we find what we seek every day,
The mosaic of life leading us on our way.

Textures of laughter, the warmth of a touch,
Weaving experiences, we cherish so much.
In moments assembled, the big and the small,
Together they form the grandest of all.

Through portraits of people, through whispers of air,
Mosaics of meaning, a tapestry fair.
Each tile intertwines in perfect refrain,
The art of existence, our beautiful chain.

Layers of Serenity

Veils of the morning, mist gently rise,
Whispers of dawn greet the waking skies.
Each layer unfolding, revealing the light,
In the hush of the moment, everything feels right.

Soft sands of the shore, secrets they keep,
Cradled by ocean's lull, quietly deep.
Waves crashing softly, like the heart's embrace,
In layers of serenity, we find our place.

Mountains stand tall, draped in drifts of snow,
Nature's calm hand guides the life below.
The rustle of leaves sings a tranquil song,
In these layers of bliss, we simply belong.

Time flows like water, steady and clear,
Echoes of quiet instill hope, not fear.
Through each gentle layer, we find our way,
Embracing the stillness as night turns to day.

Foundations of Dreams

Footsteps of hope tread soft on the ground,
Building the pathways where dreams can be found.
Brick by brick, with each breath we take,
Foundations of dreams, a future we make.

Visions arise from the heart's deep core,
Mapping the unknown, we yearn to explore.
With courage as our guide through shadows of doubt,
We weave our intentions, carving them out.

Skyward we reach for the stars up high,
Grounded in strength, with wings we can fly.
The pulse of ambition beats deep in our chest,
In foundations of dreams, we find our rest.

As night drapes gently over all that we've wrought,
We anchor our visions in each sacred thought.
For with every dawn, there's a chance to revive,
In the heart of our dreams, we truly arrive.

The Breath of Bridges

Across the river, shadows fall,
Silent whispers, the night does call.
Wood and steel in twilight glow,
Connecting worlds, they ebb and flow.

Windswept tales of journeys grand,
Footsteps echo on ancient sand.
Each plank holds stories, rich and deep,
A promise made, a vow to keep.

Clouds drift softly, the moon takes flight,
Guiding lovers through the night.
In the stillness, hearts entwine,
Bridges breathe, a sacred sign.

As the dawn breaks, light cascades,
Through every creak, the past invades.
Yet still they stand, unwavering grace,
The breath of bridges, time's embrace.

Versatile Vaults

In the heart of stone, secrets sleep,
Whispers echo, the shadows creep.
Vaults that hold the past's embrace,
Guarding dreams in timeless space.

Echoes of laughter, sighs of pain,
Stories marked by joy and rain.
Versatile, they hold the weight,
Of hopes and fears, of love and fate.

Underneath the archway grand,
Dreams collide and destinies stand.
Each stone a testament to time,
A silent rhythm, a hidden rhyme.

Walls that breathe, endure, and mold,
Treasures of the young and old.
In the silence, life unfolds,
Versatile vaults, with stories told.

Chiseled Shadows

On the canvas of the night,
Shadows dance in soft moonlight.
Carved by dreams, they twist and turn,
In every corner, secrets burn.

Figures loom, both brave and frail,
Echoes of stories woven pale.
Chiseled forms that time has shaped,
In fleeting moments, life escaped.

Fingers trace the air so light,
Sketching visions, igniting flight.
Shadows whisper, tales untold,
In their silence, hearts grow bold.

When the dawn begins to creep,
Chiseled shadows softly weep.
Yet in their ache, a beauty flourished,
In forgotten realms, dreams are nourished.

Caretakers of the Cosmos

Beneath the stars, we watch and wait,
Guardians of our shared fate.
Hands outstretched to the endless night,
Caretakers of the cosmic light.

Dreams collide in the astral sea,
Threads of time, a tapestry.
Galaxies whisper through the void,
In every heartbeat, love deployed.

Comets blaze with tales untold,
Chasing dreams of the brave and bold.
Each twinkling star holds a spark,
In the darkness, we leave our mark.

Together we rise, hand in hand,
Crafting futures, a brighter land.
Caretakers of cosmic ages,
In our hearts, the universe engages.

Foundations of Thought

In quiet corners, ideas bloom,
Roots intertwine in the mind's room.
Whispers of wisdom, softly spoken,
Building the bridges that won't be broken.

Each thought a brick, laid with care,
Crafting a structure, lofty and rare.
In the depths where questions thrive,
Foundations strengthen, keeping dreams alive.

Voices echo in an empty space,
Chasing shadows, a silent race.
Every notion, a spark of light,
Guiding the soul through the endless night.

So let us ponder, let us create,
For in our thoughts, we shape our fate.
With every question, a path unfolds,
In the foundations where meaning molds.

Skyline Serenade

As daylight fades, the skyline glows,
City lights dance in a rhythmic pose.
Steel and glass rise to touch the stars,
Whispers of dreams from the fading cars.

Each heartbeat echoes through the street,
A serenade where shadows meet.
Voices linger in the evening air,
Each note a story, woven with care.

Windows shimmer like starlit eyes,
Reflecting hopes and whispered sighs.
In the neon glow, life pulses bright,
Painting the canvas of the night.

Under the moon, the skyline sings,
A harmony born of countless things.
As we inhabit this urban dream,
The city, alive, flows like a stream.

Mosaic of Moments

Fragments of time, both lost and found,
In patterns and colors, the joy is unbound.
Each moment a tile in a grand design,
A tapestry woven with threads divine.

Laughter and tears, side by side,
In the mosaic where memories abide.
Joyful whispers and silent cries,
Every piece tells a story, never lies.

Together we stand, both weak and strong,
In a world that sways to our own song.
Each glance a brushstroke, each touch a hue,
Creating a portrait, vivid and true.

In this collage of life, we see,
The beauty of chaos, the grace of the free.
A dance of existence, a colorful blend,
In the mosaic of moments, we transcend.

Celestial Structures

Stars are the dreams that light the way,
Guiding our hearts where the shadows play.
Galaxies swirl in a cosmic dance,
A structure of wonder, a timeless romance.

Nebulas whisper in colors bright,
Crafting formations in the deep night.
Each comet's tail a fleeting sign,
Across the cosmos, the heavens align.

Constellations weave stories above,
Mapping the skies with light and love.
In the void where silence reigns,
Ancient wisdom forever remains.

So let us gaze at the stellar tapestry,
Finding our place in the galaxy.
In celestial structures, dreams take flight,
Eternally bound in the embrace of night.

Tapestry of Shadows

In the dim light, whispers weave,
Threads of night begin to grieve.
Silken forms, a dance so slow,
Beneath the moon's soft silver glow.

Fingers trace where silence grows,
In inky depths, the mystery flows.
Shadows stretch, they intertwine,
A fabric rich, both dark and fine.

Each flicker tells a tale anew,
Of dreams and fears, of dark and blue.
In their embrace, we find our peace,
Where thoughts unravel, and time may cease.

Beneath the stars, a whispered call,
In this tapestry, we rise and fall.
Lose ourselves in the night's embrace,
A fleeting touch in hidden space.

Fragments of Form

Shattered pieces, lost and found,
In every crack, a story's sound.
Fragments glimmer, reflecting light,
In chaos born, a form takes flight.

Shapes that mingle, then break apart,
A mosaic blooms within the heart.
Curved and jagged, sharp yet round,
Each fragment speaks where peace is crowned.

From the rubble, beauty breaks,
In every loss, a chance it makes.
A cycle endless, crafted anew,
In the ruins, creation brews.

Hold these pieces, cherish their grace,
In their unity, we find our place.
Every fracture, a bridge to soar,
Embrace the chaos, seek the core.

Choreography of Space

In every corner, silence spins,
The dance of shadows, where it begins.
Echoes sway, alive in the air,
A rhythm born from whispered care.

Steps unfurl across the floor,
Mapping journeys, seeking more.
Between the walls, a heartbeat plays,
In the stillness, time delays.

Curves of movement, soft and wide,
In the spaces, dreams abide.
Laughter lingers, soft as a sigh,
In every breath, we learn to fly.

This choreography, art defined,
In each flow, our hearts aligned.
Beneath the stars, we find our pace,
In the gravitas of open space.

Echoes in the Archway

Underneath the ancient stone,
Whispers wander, soft as bone.
Through the arch, a tale returns,
Of light and shadow, wisdom burns.

Moments caught in time's embrace,
In this archway, find your place.
Echoes linger, voices meet,
In every footstep, history's beat.

Carved in grace, the past resides,
In echoes sweet, where truth abides.
A passage leads, a journey starts,
Through open doors, into our hearts.

Listen closely, hear the call,
In the archway, we stand tall.
With every echo, dreams awake,
In this passage, new paths we make.

Crescendos in Columns

Whispers rise in silent halls,
Each echo's dance, a melody calls.
Columns stand, a timeless grace,
In their shadows, dreams embrace.

Life unfolds in measured beats,
Stories captured in stone seats.
Notes of laughter, tears of strife,
Within these walls, we find our life.

Moments layered, chants entwined,
A harmony through space defined.
Crescendos build, then softly fade,
In the heart of art, unafraid.

Together bound, we seek our sound,
In structures deep, our souls are found.
Each column holds a tale of yore,
A symphony forevermore.

Textures of Time

Worn pages whisper tales of old,
In fragile threads, the past unfolds.
Textures rich, in layers lie,
Each moment caught, a silent sigh.

Grains of sand slip through our hands,
Yet in their fall, a wisdom stands.
Time's embrace, both gentle, cruel,
In every heartbeat, we find the rule.

Seasons change with fleeting grace,
Marks of life, we cannot erase.
In tender hues, the hours blend,
A canvas rich, we apprehend.

Through woven dreams, we navigate,
The textures spun by love and fate.
In every fold, a story gleams,
Time's tapestry, our woven dreams.

Skylines and Sonnets

Against the dawn, the skyline glows,
Each building stacks, where sunlight flows.
A wish upon the fading light,
In concrete stillness, day meets night.

Lines of verse in shadows dance,
Each sonnet born from chance romance.
Above the city, stars are penned,
In every breath, new hopes ascend.

Glass and steel, they pierce the sky,
Yet through the heights, our spirits fly.
Within these forms, our voices rise,
A harmony beneath the skies.

From rooftops high, our dreams ignite,
With sonnets shining through the night.
A skyline forged with words divine,
In every heart, a secret sign.

The Art of Structure

Each line a beam, each word a brace,
In language carved, we find our place.
The art of structure, firm yet free,
A framework built for you and me.

Verses rise like arching spans,
Bridging thoughts across the lands.
In every stanza, a heartbeat flows,
A garden where the meaning grows.

Foundations laid in subtle tones,
In written realms, we're not alone.
The craft of lines, both loose and tight,
Creates a dance of pure delight.

With every phrase, we build anew,
A world where dreams can come true.
The art of structure, bold and bright,
In every shadow, we find light.

Reflections in Reinforcement

In shadows cast by steel and stone,
We find the strength we often own.
The beams that rise, a story shared,
Within their bonds, our hopes declared.

Through cracks and lines, our dreams unfold,
Each fracture speaks of tales retold.
Echoes linger in the halls,
Of whispered thoughts within these walls.

As sunlight dances on the frame,
Reflections twist, yet still the same.
Foundation firm, with grace we stand,
In every arch, a guiding hand.

From depths of strength, we rise anew,
Crafting futures from the view.
With every pulse, our spirits bind,
A testament to hearts aligned.

The Soul of Structures

Beyond the bricks and iron might,
Lies something pure, a guiding light.
In every curve, the soul does weave,
An essence found in what we believe.

The arches speak of dreams unchained,
In every silence, passion gained.
Columns stand like ancient trees,
Guardians of whispered memories.

Windows frame the world outside,
Reflecting hopes we cannot hide.
Through solid walls, a warmth flows deep,
A sanctuary where visions sleep.

Each layer holds a tale untold,
In shadows cast, our truths unfold.
Structures breathe with life anew,
In every heartbeat, we construe.

Balance of Beams

In harmony the beams align,
A dance of strength, a bold design.
We weave our dreams in timber's grace,
Creating space where hopes embrace.

Through tension's pull and gravity's claim,
Each element plays a sacred game.
With every joint, a story spins,
A testament to where it begins.

As forces meet, the balance sways,
In perfect poise, the structure stays.
The framework stands both firm and free,
A symbol of our unity.

Together bound, we rise and soar,
In symmetry, we seek for more.
A harmony of hearts combined,
In every beam, our dreams aligned.

Echoed Emotions

In walls that listen, secrets hum,
A chorus soft, a heart's own drum.
The laughter lingers in the breeze,
An echo stirs among the trees.

Through corridors, the whispers glide,
Each memory, an ebbing tide.
With every step, we trace the past,
The echoes weave, forever cast.

In silence strong, our feelings grow,
Reflections dance in twilight's glow.
The structures hold our tales entwined,
In every nook, a love defined.

As shadows stretch and daylight fades,
The echoes linger in the shades.
In every space, the heart's refrain,
A symphony of joy and pain.

Echoes of Stone

Ancient walls hold tales untold,
Secrets whispered in the cold.
Every crack, a story spun,
Beneath the weight of time, we run.

Chiseled paths that we have walked,
In the silence, spirits talked.
Granite dreams of ages past,
Echoes linger, shadows cast.

Through the arches, light does creep,
Calling forth the souls in sleep.
In the stillness, hear their song,
In the heart of stone, we belong.

With each step, a memory found,
In the echoes, we're unbound.
Stone may fade and crumble down,
But the echoes wear the crown.

Dreams in Concrete

Beneath the towers, visions rise,
In the hardscape, hope defies.
Dreams are poured in every lane,
Amidst the hustle, joy and pain.

Grey horizons stretch so wide,
City heartbeats, side by side.
Concrete jungles, life unfolds,
In their shadow, stories told.

Each sidewalk bears the weight of feet,
Journeys started, paths repeat.
Underneath the urban sway,
We weave our dreams from day to day.

In the stillness of the night,
Stars reflect the city's light.
Concrete blooms with dreams anew,
Reminding us of skies so blue.

Whispers of Wooden Beams

Gentle creaks in twilight's glow,
Wooden hearts that ebb and flow.
Timber tales from quiet nights,
In their grain, the warmth ignites.

Branches sway, a soft caress,
Whispers wrapped in nature's dress.
Every knot a life embraced,
In the still, their grace is traced.

Rustle under moonlit frames,
Life in wood, it softly claims.
Nestled dreams in beams so strong,
Where the souls of trees belong.

Echoes of the forest sing,
In the beams, the memories cling.
Nature's touch, a tender seam,
Binding us within the dream.

Symphonies of Steel

In the clash, the forging sound,
Strength and beauty, tightly wound.
Shimmering beams against the sky,
In their rise, our spirits fly.

Rhythms echo in the night,
Steel and iron dance with light.
A testament to dreams made real,
Crafted notes, we dare to feel.

Structures soaring, reaching high,
Against the clouds, we learn to fly.
In the city's vibrant beat,
Life flows on, relentless, sweet.

Every structure tells a tale,
In the wind, we set the sail.
Steel's embrace, a steadfast ground,
In its strength, our dreams are found.

Horizons of Harmony

In the dawn's soft glow, we rise,
With dreams that dance across the skies,
Unity whispers in the breeze,
Harmony flows through swaying trees.

In every heart, a song does swell,
With notes of peace and tales to tell,
As colors blend in vibrant light,
We find our joy in shared delight.

The ocean sings, the mountains call,
Together bound, we rise and fall,
A symphony of voices strong,
In this embrace, we all belong.

Let love be our guiding star,
No matter how near or far,
Together, we can make a change,
In horizons vast, we can rearrange.

The Story in the Stairs

Each step we take, a tale unfolds,
Of whispered dreams and secrets told,
The creak of wood beneath our feet,
Echoes of memories bittersweet.

Handrails worn from loving hands,
A journey crafted by our plans,
Through laughter shared and tears we've cried,
In every rise, our hope and pride.

The golden light that softly glows,
Illuminates where passion flows,
In shadows deep, the moments sway,
A staircase leads us on our way.

With every step, we come alive,
In stories written, we survive,
Each flight a chance to pause or climb,
In the heart of stairs, we hold our time.

Traces of Tradition

In woven threads, our stories blend,
Ancestors' voices never end,
Passed through hands, a sacred bond,
Crafting legacies, a silent song.

The dance of seasons marks our days,
In rituals, we find our ways,
From feast to fast, from birth to mourn,
In every cycle, hope is born.

The flavors rich, the echoes dine,
On tables set, in hearts entwined,
Wisdom flows from elders wise,
In every heart, tradition lies.

With every tale, we etch a line,
A tapestry of love so fine,
Traces left for those who seek,
In heritage, our spirits speak.

The Metaphor of Material

The glass reflects a world so bright,
Yet hides the shadows of our plight,
In metal's strength, we seek to find,
The weight of dreams, the ties that bind.

In fabric soft, we stitch our fears,
Each thread a tale of laughter, tears,
The jewels we wear, a hint of pride,
Yet deeper truths we oft confide.

Crumbled paper holds a thought,
In every nuance, battles fought,
The stones we stack, a tower tall,
Are monuments to rise and fall.

Through all we build, with heart and hand,
The metaphors in life, we stand,
To seek the deeper, hidden core,
In every piece, we aim for more.

Narrative in the Nook

In the quiet corner, stories lie,
Whispers of ages pass by the eye.
Books stacked high, dreams take their flight,
Each spine a journey, hidden from light.

A chair worn down, cradles thoughts,
A world within, where time forgot.
The dust motes dance in beams of gold,
Each tale unfolds, waiting to be told.

Faded photographs, memories cling,
Echoes of laughter, the joy they bring.
In this nook, time gently bends,
A lighthouse of love that never ends.

With every turn of a weathered page,
Life's mosaics blend, age to age.
In the shadows, stories entwined,
A sanctuary where hearts align.

Luminescent Layers

Beneath the surface, colors glow,
Layers of life, ebb and flow.
Shimmers of dreams, bright and clear,
In this tapestry, we hold dear.

Echoes of joy, whispers of pain,
Each thread woven, a refrain.
Under the light, shadows reveal,
Truths in layers that time can steal.

In the garden of thoughts, seeds we sow,
Like petals unfolding, they teach us to grow.
Through storms and sunshine, we find our way,
Luminescent layers guide our stay.

With every dawn, new hues ignite,
Life's canvas painted, morning light.
Each layer a story, rich and grand,
In the heart's gallery, we take our stand.

The Music of Mankind's Hands

With calloused palms, we craft and create,
Rhythms arise, hearts resonate.
Fingers dance on strings of time,
In every note, a pulse, a rhyme.

Hands that toil, hands that play,
Weaving together the night and day.
In factories, fields, under the sun,
The music of hands, a journey begun.

Each heartbeat echoes, resonant sound,
In unity's chorus, we are found.
From the craftsman's hammer to the pianist's chords,
Life's symphony plays, a harmony of lords.

Through laughter and tears, together we stand,
In the orchestra formed by humanity's hand.
With every creation, a story unfolds,
The music of mankind, in our hearts, it holds.

Harmony in Hardscape

Amidst the concrete, life finds a way,
Roots break through gaps, dance and sway.
Pavements tell tales of footsteps worn,
In the urban breath, nature is reborn.

Skyscrapers rise, towers of glass,
Mirroring dreams that refuse to pass.
In shadows cast, there's beauty found,
Harmony whispers, in silence profound.

With each sunrise, colors converge,
Skyline embraces nature's urge.
Art in the alleys, bricks infused,
In hardscape's heart, life's rhythm is mused.

Under the stars, city lights gleam,
Together they weave, a luminous dream.
In the symphony of stone and soul,
Harmony's promise makes us whole.